DIVORCE

CAN HAPPEN TO THE NICEST PEOPLE.

By Peter Mayle

Illustrated by Arthur Robins

Macmillan Publishing Co. Inc.
New York

For Ernie, Michael and Mavis,
with many thanks.

Text copyright©1979 by Peter Mayle. Illustrations copyright©1979 by Arthur Robins.
Designed by Martin Reavley. Typography by Maggie Lewis.

Macmillan Publishing Co. Inc. 866 Third Avenue, New York N.Y. 10022.
Library of Congress No. 79-93006
Printed in the United States of America.

9   8   7   6   5   4   3   2   1

ISBN   0-02-582500-3

Old people, young people, rich people, poor people....

Do you know how many people in the world get divorced each year?

The last time anybody counted, which was in 1976, it was more than six million.

Old people, young people, rich people, poor people, black people, white people, people from Alaska and people from Africa–more than one hundred thousand every day decided that they would be happier living apart than living together.

More people get divorced in one day than you could fit into Yankee Stadium.

More people get divorced in one year than the entire population of Ireland.

More people get divorced each year than the entire population of Ireland.

And yet, strangely enough when you think how many times it happens, divorce is often treated like some rare and awful disease. Something to be whispered about. Something to be ashamed of. As though there was something wrong with the people who get divorced.

When you stop to think about it, that's nonsense. Nothing that happens millions of times a year can be called rare. And six million people can't be all bad, just because they get divorced.

In fact, most of them are normal, nice men and women. Like your parents, for instance.

Divorce is very sad, but it's a fact of life. And the first thing you should try to understand is that you're not a freak if it happens in your family.

Your parents aren't monsters. You're not even very unusual as a family. You're just unlucky.

You know how you're always being told that you must do this or you must do that? Well, it's different when you're trying to understand divorce. It's the mustn'ts that are important. And these three are the most important.

You mustn't make the mistake of thinking that your parents don't love you because they're getting divorced.

You mustn't think that the whole thing is somehow your fault, because it never is.

And you mustn't put the blame on one parent, because divorce is never really only one person's fault.

Like anything else in life, divorce is easier to cope with if you have some idea of why it happens. And that's what we're going to try to explain in this book.

But perhaps we should start at the beginning. Because you can't have a divorce unless you have first had a marriage.

You mustn't think that the whole thing is somehow your fault —

WHY YOUR PARENTS GOT MARRIED.

With all those hundreds of thousands of divorces every year, you may wonder why anybody should want to get married in the first place.

Let's take your mother and father as an example, and see what happened with them.

A long time ago, long before you, they met each other and liked each other. And the more they saw of each other, the more they wanted to be together. One date a week turned into three or four dates a week. Before long, they were seeing each other every day.

This next part may be hard for you to believe now, but your mother and father fell in love. They wanted to be together all the time. They wanted to share a bed. They wanted to share a home. They wanted to share a whole life. They hated the idea of being away from each other.

When you feel like that, living in separate houses is no fun at all. So they decided to live together.

Why didn't they leave it at that? After all, there are plenty of men and women who live together without being married. Why couldn't your parents have done the same?

If you had asked them that question at the time, they would probably have told you that they wanted to have children. That they wanted to be one family instead of two people. And in our society, the way to make that official is to get married.

A long time ago,
long before you,
they met each other
and liked each other

Marriage tells everybody in the world what the man and the woman have been telling each other. It takes their private promise and turns it into a public, legal agreement.

The tradition of men and women being married before they start to have children goes back a long, long way. The first people to have their weddings written about were the Greeks, and that was three thousand years ago. The fact that people are still getting married today proves that it's a tradition that most men and women like.

Getting married shows that the man and the woman are prepared to do their best to stay together, and to raise their children together. Perhaps that sounds very obvious to you, but it doesn't always happen the same way among other living things.

Birds, for instance, don't have much of a family life. Often, father bird won't ever see his own babies; the mother raises them on her own.

Birds for instance
don't have much of a
family life

And after quite a short time – just a few weeks – even mother's had enough. The young ones are given a friendly shove and told to go and take care of themselves. That's the way it is with dogs, or cats, or most other animals. The idea of a family as we know it hardly exists.

The two big differences with people.....

The two big differences with people are that both parents help to raise the children, and the children are often young adults before they leave home. They might have as much as twenty years of living with their parents before going into the world on their own.

As you're finding out, it doesn't always work that way. But don't ever think that your parents got married with the idea of getting divorced later. It wouldn't make sense. Everyone who gets married believes that it will last.

The truly sad thing is that two people can try very hard to stay happily married, but still end up divorced. And if you think that sounds crazy, wait till you read about some of the things people have said were reasons for divorce in the past.

but still end up divorced —

WHAT GOES WRONG?

There are two sizes of reasons why people get divorced. The big reason–which we come to in a minute–and an assortment of smaller reasons, some serious and some silly.

Here are just a few:

"He snores so loud I can't sleep."

"She always leaves the top off the toothpaste."

… leaving the cap off the toothpaste —

"He hides behind the newspaper at breakfast."

"She smokes in bed."

"He's always leaving the toilet seat up."

"She reads my mail."

"He reads *my* mail."

They're more like complaints, really. And they're not very important, as you can see. But they become bigger and more important and more annoying when two people aren't happy living with each other. What you find sweet and funny when you love someone can drive you crazy when you don't.

And that's the real reason for divorce: not enough love. Just as two people can fall in love, they can fall out of love too. And just as it's hard to live apart from someone you love, it's very hard to live with someone you don't.

"She smokes in bed."

Nobody has ever been able to say exactly what it is that makes one person fall in love with another. It's a complicated mixture of feelings and needs and likes and dislikes that are totally different from person to person.

What it is that makes people fall *out* of love, though, is a little easier to understand.

Think back a couple of years. Can you remember what you best liked doing then? And the friends you liked to be with?

Do you still like everything you liked then? Do you still see the same people? The chances are that without really noticing it, you're different now from the way you were then. You've changed.

Adults are supposed to have got through most of their changing by the time they get married. But the truth is that people don't stand still, no matter how old they are. All of us change all through our lives.

And that's where problems can start. Everyone changes in different ways and at different speeds. With luck, you and the person you're married to can adjust to the changes that are going on. But sometimes they come along so fast or they can be so big that suddenly it's like being married to someone you hardly know.

When that happens, it makes living together more and more difficult. Both people become unhappy. Those silly little habits like leaving the cap off the toothpaste tube and falling asleep in front of the TV gradually get more and more

Do you still
    like everything you liked then?

annoying. You look for excuses to be apart. You spend less and less time together. Then one day, you have to admit that with all the trying in the world, the marriage just won't work.

If there are no children involved, it's easier to agree that the marriage was a sad mistake, and the best thing is for both of you to go your separate ways.

But when there are children, it's much much harder. Do you stay together and pretend to be happy, and hope that the kids won't notice? Or do you split up, so that each of you has the chance to be happy with someone else?

Your mother and father have decided to split up. They thought about it and worried about you before they decided. But their hope is that they and you will be happier in the long run because of what they've done. It's hard to believe that now, but wait and see. You'll probably find they were right.

— their hope is that they and you will be happier in the long run —

OTHER MEN AND OTHER WOMEN.

As if there weren't already plenty of reasons why people get divorced, here's one more. And it's important enough to tell you about separately.

It usually happens when the mother and the father are going through some changes and having all their troubles. Right out of the blue, one of them meets and falls in love with someone else.

More problems, more complications, more sadness. It's sad and difficult for everyone.

If you're the parent who has fallen in love with someone else, it's one of the hardest things in the world to tell your children.

If you're the other parent, you feel more lonely and unhappy than ever.

If you're one of the children, it's not easy to accept someone else as a brand new parent.

And if you're the someone else, it's hard because you know you're making everything more difficult for everybody.

Nobody plans it, but that's the way it often is. We'd like to be able to say that there's an overnight remedy for all this unhappiness and confusion, but there isn't. The only cure that really works is time.

.... It's better than living with two unhappy parents—

LIVING WITH HALF YOUR PARENTS.

In time, you'll find that living with one more or less happy parent is better than living with two unhappy parents. But nobody could say that the first few months of this new kind of life are easy.

No matter how much you might feel you want to, you can't split yourself in two. So you have to get used to living with one parent and visiting the other. And to begin with, there may not be too many visits; divorced people often get very angry with each other, and need time apart to calm down.

When parents divorce, it's usually (but not always) the father who leaves home. And until you understand why, you're bound to think he doesn't love you as much as your mother does. How could he? He's walked out and left you.

There are two good reasons why your father goes and your mother stays.

First, the family home should be for the family. It would be very unfair if your father took the home just for himself and made everyone else go and look for another place to live.

The second reason is that your mother, even if she goes out to work, is probably a lot better at looking after you and the home than your father is. Mothers usually are. (Your father may be a great cook and a genius at ironing, but most fathers aren't.)

a genius at ironing,
but most fathers aren't

You see? Neither of those reasons has anything to do with one parent loving you more or less than the other one does.

Once you realize that, it might help you feel a bit less sad about only being able to visit your father.

There's no instant magic way to cheer yourself up. But feeling sorry for yourself is only going to make you more miserable, which is going to make your mother and father more miserable. And if you feel that you're having a bad time, think how much worse it is for them.

Remember that your mother loves you very much. Remember that your father loves you very much. And remember that being unhappy doesn't last.

There's no instant
magic way to
cheer yourself up —

WHO'S RIGHT? WHO'S WRONG? WHO'S TO BLAME?

From the day you trip over and blame your shoelace to the day your false teeth fall in the soup and you blame your dentist, you're always looking for someone to blame when life goes wrong. It's human nature; if you're upset, it *has* to be someone else's fault.

Divorce is one of the biggest upsets there is in life. Everybody involved wants to blame somebody. And who do you see when you look around for somewhere to place the blame? Your parents. They've obviously done all this on purpose just to make you sad and angry.

You know it's not your fault, so it must be theirs. And of course, it is. But the trouble is that it's not easy to be fair when you're upset.

If you could divide the blame equally between both parents, perhaps that would make some sense. But you never can.

You might put most of the blame on your father because he's gone away and left you. You might blame your mother because she's made your father unhappy enough to leave. Nearly always, though, you find yourself taking sides with one parent, while the other one gets it in the neck.

Sadly, parents themselves often encourage this. They're upset too, and they're looking for someone to blame. Mostly, it's each other.

From the day you trip over and blame your shoelace....

It's difficult for you to be fair when neither of them is being fair. Divorced parents are often not only nasty *to* each other. They're nasty *about* each other. And you sometimes get caught in the middle of it all. It's enough to make you feel you're watching a boxing match, with words being used instead of fists.

There isn't much to be cheerful about while this is going on. All we can say is that people can't stay mad at each other forever. They calm down, and they realize that there are better things to do than spend their lives being angry.

That applies to you as well as them, so try not to get mad. Two people fighting in one family is quite enough without you joining in.

And try as hard as you can not to take sides. Remember, divorce is never just one person's fault.

And you're sometimes caught in the middle of it all.

AT LAST THE GOOD NEWS.

Divorce isn't all bad. There is a bright side, as long as you and your parents are prepared to give it a chance.

Let's say you're living with your mother and visiting your father. Even though you've known him all your life, those first visits are bound to feel strange. It's strange to see him living in a different place, maybe with somebody else, and it's strange to have to say goodbye.

After a while, you get used to the idea that divorce doesn't mean goodbye forever. And then, little by little, visit by visit, you'll begin to find that maybe life isn't so sad and bad after all. There are even one or two consolation prizes that you only get when your parents are divorced.

We're not saying that they make up for not living with both parents, but they help. For instance:

MAKING FRIENDS WITH TWO NEW PEOPLE.

When you spend time with your mother and father separately, something interesting happens. You start to see them as people rather than parents; they start to see you as a person rather than their child.

Because they aren't busy with each other, they can spend more time talking to you, listening to you, and getting to know you. This feels funny, but good. It's like finding two new friends whom you know you're going to like for a long time.

AN EXTRA LIFE.

When you lived with both your parents, you had one kind of life. Now that you're living with each parent, but separately, you have the chance of trying two lives, and they'll be very different.

Your mother will have her friends. Your father will have his. You'll meet them all.

Your mother will have her way of doing things. Your father will have his. You'll try both.

Your mother will have her special likes:	Your father will have his:
A white Christmas	Sunbathing on Christmas Eve
Going to the theater	Watching old films on TV
Hamburgers	Pizza
Walks in the rain	Breakfast in bed
Big hairy dogs	Siamese cats
Ice skating	Football
Robert Redford	Mickey Mouse

We just made up that list, but you get the idea: when you share two separate lives with two separate people, it can be very interesting. Better still, it can be a lot of fun. And that's something you never thought you'd get from a divorce.

your mother will have
her special likes:

your father will
have his:

She finds herself with a whole batch of new problems.

PARENTS NEED ALL THE HELP
THEY CAN GET.

One more time, think what getting divorced is like for your mother and father.

It's a mess. They're sad and angry and upset. They're worried about you. And on top of that, everyday life is suddenly much harder to cope with. Each of them now has to do chores that used to be shared between them.

Your mother is not only having to take care of you, and the house, and maybe a job. She now finds herself with a whole batch of new problems. If the car breaks down, she has to get it repaired. If the garden is turning into a jungle, she has to sort it out. If the neighbors are having too many noisy parties, she has to go and complain. Problems that used to be shared now have to be solved on their own.

Meanwhile, your father isn't having too good a time either. In between doing his job, and probably paying for two homes, he now has the housework: cooking, cleaning, bed making, shopping for food, organizing the laundry, doing the dishes, and generally taking care of himself. He hasn't anyone to share the chores with either.

It's no fun for either of them. But it can be a lot better for them if you make up your mind that you're going to help in every way you can.

First, you could try to forget how sad you are, and remember how sad they are. Why don't you see if you can cheer them up instead of waiting for them to cheer you up? (Telling them that you love them makes a pretty good start.)

Next, you could do your share of chores – or even a bit more than your share. Nobody's going to expect you to cook a seven-course meal while you're doing the ironing, mowing the lawn and washing the car, but there's nothing to stop your getting into a few useful habits.

If you don't already do these, tomorrow would be a great day to start: making your own bed, clearing away the dishes, tidying your own room, washing out the bath after you use it and hanging up your clothes. They're boring, perhaps. But why should someone else have to do your boring chores?

The last way you can help is much more difficult. But it's also much more important.

For most mothers and fathers, the hardest part of divorce is being worried about the children. How will they feel about their parents? Will they end up hating their mother, or their father, or both? Will they be too upset to cope with school? The list of worries goes on and on.

Now it's a fact that worries are worse when you keep them to yourself. The minute you can tell someone about them, they're somehow not quite so bad. And that's where you come in.

Parents don't find it easy to talk about divorce. They sometimes need a little nudge from you. This nudge could be asking them straight out to tell you what went wrong, or it could be showing them that you're not going to let it get you down.

How you do it doesn't matter, as long as you let them know that you're old enough and sensible enough to understand divorce and talk about it. And that you love them enough to want to help.

Do the best you can. After all, it's not often people of your age get to help people of their age.

.... And hanging up your clothes—

J
306.89   9-83
MAY   Mayle, Peter
       Divorce Can Happen to
       the Nicest People

DATE DUE			
DEC 27 198	83775		
NOV 1 4 1984	84759		
JUL 2 6 1985	83-346		
MAR - 4 1986	85116		
APR 7 1986	86144		
JUN 3 0 1986	84661		
AUG 21 1986	92-232		
SEP 8 1986	82-259		
NOV 1 1986	85-850		
FEB 1 1 1987	86144		